Monthly Profit Tracker

Month	Total Spend	Total Sales	Total Profit

Purchase & Sales Tracker

Item	Purchase Date	Sale Date	Sale Website	Purchase Price	Sale Price	Profit

Total

Purchase & Sales Tracker

DATES FROM ________________________

Item	Purchase Date	Sale Date	Sale Website	Purchase Price	Sale Price	Profit

Total

Purchase & Sales Tracker

Item	Purchase Date	Sale Date	Sale Website	Purchase Price	Sale Price	Profit

Total

Purchase & Sales Tracker

Item	Purchase Date	Sale Date	Sale Website	Purchase Price	Sale Price	Profit

Total

Purchase & Sales Tracker

DATES FROM ___________________

Item	Purchase Date	Sale Date	Sale Website	Purchase Price	Sale Price	Profit

Total

Purchase & Sales Tracker

DATES FROM ______________________

Item	Purchase Date	Sale Date	Sale Website	Purchase Price	Sale Price	Profit

Total

Purchase & Sales Tracker

Item	Purchase Date	Sale Date	Sale Website	Purchase Price	Sale Price	Profit

Total

Purchase & Sales Tracker

DATES FROM _______________

Item	Purchase Date	Sale Date	Sale Website	Purchase Price	Sale Price	Profit

Total

Purchase & Sales Tracker

DATES FROM ______________________

Item	Purchase Date	Sale Date	Sale Website	Purchase Price	Sale Price	Profit

Total

Purchase & Sales Tracker

DATES FROM ___________________________

Item	Purchase Date	Sale Date	Sale Website	Purchase Price	Sale Price	Profit

Total

Purchase & Sales Tracker

DATES FROM ______________

Item	Purchase Date	Sale Date	Sale Website	Purchase Price	Sale Price	Profit

Total | | | |

Purchase & Sales Tracker

DATES FROM _______________

Item	Purchase Date	Sale Date	Sale Website	Purchase Price	Sale Price	Profit

Total

Purchase & Sales Tracker

DATES FROM ________________

Item	Purchase Date	Sale Date	Sale Website	Purchase Price	Sale Price	Profit

Total

Purchase & Sales Tracker

DATES FROM ___________________________

Item	Purchase Date	Sale Date	Sale Website	Purchase Price	Sale Price	Profit

Total

Purchase & Sales Tracker

DATES FROM ______________________

Item	Purchase Date	Sale Date	Sale Website	Purchase Price	Sale Price	Profit

Total

Purchase & Sales Tracker

DATES FROM ___________________________

Item	Purchase Date	Sale Date	Sale Website	Purchase Price	Sale Price	Profit

Total | | | |

Purchase & Sales Tracker

DATES FROM _______________

Item	Purchase Date	Sale Date	Sale Website	Purchase Price	Sale Price	Profit

Total

Purchase & Sales Tracker

DATES FROM ______________________

Item	Purchase Date	Sale Date	Sale Website	Purchase Price	Sale Price	Profit

Total

Purchase & Sales Tracker

DATES FROM _______________

Item	Purchase Date	Sale Date	Sale Website	Purchase Price	Sale Price	Profit

Total | | | |

Purchase & Sales Tracker

DATES FROM _______________

Item	Purchase Date	Sale Date	Sale Website	Purchase Price	Sale Price	Profit

Total | | | |

Purchase & Sales Tracker

DATES FROM ______________________

Item	Purchase Date	Sale Date	Sale Website	Purchase Price	Sale Price	Profit

Total

Purchase & Sales Tracker

DATES FROM ___________________

Item	Purchase Date	Sale Date	Sale Website	Purchase Price	Sale Price	Profit

Total

Purchase & Sales Tracker

DATES FROM ________________

Item	Purchase Date	Sale Date	Sale Website	Purchase Price	Sale Price	Profit

Total

Purchase & Sales Tracker

DATES FROM ___________________

Item	Purchase Date	Sale Date	Sale Website	Purchase Price	Sale Price	Profit

Total ________ ________ ________

Purchase & Sales Tracker

DATES FROM _______________

Item	Purchase Date	Sale Date	Sale Website	Purchase Price	Sale Price	Profit

Total

Purchase & Sales Tracker

DATES FROM ________________

Item	Purchase Date	Sale Date	Sale Website	Purchase Price	Sale Price	Profit

Total

Purchase & Sales Tracker

DATES FROM ______________

Item	Purchase Date	Sale Date	Sale Website	Purchase Price	Sale Price	Profit

Total

Purchase & Sales Tracker

DATES FROM ________________

Item	Purchase Date	Sale Date	Sale Website	Purchase Price	Sale Price	Profit

Total

Purchase & Sales Tracker

DATES FROM _______________

Item	Purchase Date	Sale Date	Sale Website	Purchase Price	Sale Price	Profit

Total

Purchase & Sales Tracker

Item	Purchase Date	Sale Date	Sale Website	Purchase Price	Sale Price	Profit

Total

Purchase & Sales Tracker

DATES FROM ________________________

Item	Purchase Date	Sale Date	Sale Website	Purchase Price	Sale Price	Profit

Total

Purchase & Sales Tracker

Item	Purchase Date	Sale Date	Sale Website	Purchase Price	Sale Price	Profit

Total

Purchase & Sales Tracker

DATES FROM ________________

Item	Purchase Date	Sale Date	Sale Website	Purchase Price	Sale Price	Profit

Total

Purchase & Sales Tracker

Item	Purchase Date	Sale Date	Sale Website	Purchase Price	Sale Price	Profit

Total

Purchase & Sales Tracker

DATES FROM ______________________

Item	Purchase Date	Sale Date	Sale Website	Purchase Price	Sale Price	Profit

Total

Purchase & Sales Tracker

DATES FROM ______________

Item	Purchase Date	Sale Date	Sale Website	Purchase Price	Sale Price	Profit

Total

Purchase & Sales Tracker

DATES FROM ________________

Item	Purchase Date	Sale Date	Sale Website	Purchase Price	Sale Price	Profit

Total | | |

Purchase & Sales Tracker

DATES FROM ______________________

Item	Purchase Date	Sale Date	Sale Website	Purchase Price	Sale Price	Profit

Total

Purchase & Sales Tracker

DATES FROM ___________

Item	Purchase Date	Sale Date	Sale Website	Purchase Price	Sale Price	Profit

Total

Purchase & Sales Tracker

DATES FROM ___________

Item	Purchase Date	Sale Date	Sale Website	Purchase Price	Sale Price	Profit

Total | | |

Purchase & Sales Tracker

DATES FROM _______________

Item	Purchase Date	Sale Date	Sale Website	Purchase Price	Sale Price	Profit

Total

Purchase & Sales Tracker

DATES FROM ___________________

Item	Purchase Date	Sale Date	Sale Website	Purchase Price	Sale Price	Profit

Total

Purchase & Sales Tracker

DATES FROM _______________

Item	Purchase Date	Sale Date	Sale Website	Purchase Price	Sale Price	Profit

Total _______________

Purchase & Sales Tracker

DATES FROM ___________________________

Item	Purchase Date	Sale Date	Sale Website	Purchase Price	Sale Price	Profit

Total

Purchase & Sales Tracker

Item	Purchase Date	Sale Date	Sale Website	Purchase Price	Sale Price	Profit

Total

Purchase & Sales Tracker

DATES FROM ___________________

Item	Purchase Date	Sale Date	Sale Website	Purchase Price	Sale Price	Profit

Total

Purchase & Sales Tracker

DATES FROM ________________

Item	Purchase Date	Sale Date	Sale Website	Purchase Price	Sale Price	Profit

Total

Purchase & Sales Tracker

DATES FROM ______________________

Item	Purchase Date	Sale Date	Sale Website	Purchase Price	Sale Price	Profit

Total | | |

Purchase & Sales Tracker

DATES FROM ___________________

Item	Purchase Date	Sale Date	Sale Website	Purchase Price	Sale Price	Profit

Total | | | |

Purchase & Sales Tracker

DATES FROM ________________

Item	Purchase Date	Sale Date	Sale Website	Purchase Price	Sale Price	Profit

Total [ ] [ ] [ ]

Purchase & Sales Tracker

DATES FROM ______________________

Item	Purchase Date	Sale Date	Sale Website	Purchase Price	Sale Price	Profit

Total

Purchase & Sales Tracker

DATES FROM ___________________

Item	Purchase Date	Sale Date	Sale Website	Purchase Price	Sale Price	Profit

Total

Purchase & Sales Tracker

DATES FROM ______________________

Item	Purchase Date	Sale Date	Sale Website	Purchase Price	Sale Price	Profit

Total

Purchase & Sales Tracker

DATES FROM ___________________

Item	Purchase Date	Sale Date	Sale Website	Purchase Price	Sale Price	Profit

Total

Purchase & Sales Tracker

Item	Purchase Date	Sale Date	Sale Website	Purchase Price	Sale Price	Profit

Total

Purchase & Sales Tracker

Item	Purchase Date	Sale Date	Sale Website	Purchase Price	Sale Price	Profit

Total

Purchase & Sales Tracker

Item	Purchase Date	Sale Date	Sale Website	Purchase Price	Sale Price	Profit

Total

Purchase & Sales Tracker

DATES FROM ______________

Item	Purchase Date	Sale Date	Sale Website	Purchase Price	Sale Price	Profit

Total

Purchase & Sales Tracker

DATES FROM _______________

Item	Purchase Date	Sale Date	Sale Website	Purchase Price	Sale Price	Profit

Total | | | |

Purchase & Sales Tracker

DATES FROM ______________

Item	Purchase Date	Sale Date	Sale Website	Purchase Price	Sale Price	Profit

Total

Purchase & Sales Tracker

DATES FROM ______________________________

Item	Purchase Date	Sale Date	Sale Website	Purchase Price	Sale Price	Profit

Total

Purchase & Sales Tracker

DATES FROM __________________

Item	Purchase Date	Sale Date	Sale Website	Purchase Price	Sale Price	Profit

Total

Purchase & Sales Tracker

DATES FROM ___________________

Item	Purchase Date	Sale Date	Sale Website	Purchase Price	Sale Price	Profit

Total

Purchase & Sales Tracker

DATES FROM _______________

Item	Purchase Date	Sale Date	Sale Website	Purchase Price	Sale Price	Profit

Total | | | |

Purchase & Sales Tracker

DATES FROM _______________

Item	Purchase Date	Sale Date	Sale Website	Purchase Price	Sale Price	Profit

Total

Purchase & Sales Tracker

DATES FROM _____________

Item	Purchase Date	Sale Date	Sale Website	Purchase Price	Sale Price	Profit

Total

Purchase & Sales Tracker

DATES FROM ______________________

Item	Purchase Date	Sale Date	Sale Website	Purchase Price	Sale Price	Profit

Total | | |

Purchase & Sales Tracker

DATES FROM ________________

Item	Purchase Date	Sale Date	Sale Website	Purchase Price	Sale Price	Profit

Total

Purchase & Sales Tracker

DATES FROM ___________________

Item	Purchase Date	Sale Date	Sale Website	Purchase Price	Sale Price	Profit

Total

Purchase & Sales Tracker

DATES FROM _______________________

Item	Purchase Date	Sale Date	Sale Website	Purchase Price	Sale Price	Profit

Total

Purchase & Sales Tracker

DATES FROM _______________________

Item	Purchase Date	Sale Date	Sale Website	Purchase Price	Sale Price	Profit

Total

Purchase & Sales Tracker

DATES FROM ______________________

Item	Purchase Date	Sale Date	Sale Website	Purchase Price	Sale Price	Profit

Total

Purchase & Sales Tracker

DATES FROM ______________

Item	Purchase Date	Sale Date	Sale Website	Purchase Price	Sale Price	Profit

Total

Purchase & Sales Tracker

DATES FROM ________________________

Item	Purchase Date	Sale Date	Sale Website	Purchase Price	Sale Price	Profit

Total

Purchase & Sales Tracker

DATES FROM ______________________

Item	Purchase Date	Sale Date	Sale Website	Purchase Price	Sale Price	Profit

Total

Purchase & Sales Tracker

DATES FROM ______________________

Item	Purchase Date	Sale Date	Sale Website	Purchase Price	Sale Price	Profit

Total | | | |

Purchase & Sales Tracker

DATES FROM ______________

Item	Purchase Date	Sale Date	Sale Website	Purchase Price	Sale Price	Profit

Total

Purchase & Sales Tracker

DATES FROM ________________

Item	Purchase Date	Sale Date	Sale Website	Purchase Price	Sale Price	Profit

Total

Purchase & Sales Tracker

DATES FROM ________________________

Item	Purchase Date	Sale Date	Sale Website	Purchase Price	Sale Price	Profit

Total

Purchase & Sales Tracker

DATES FROM _______________

Item	Purchase Date	Sale Date	Sale Website	Purchase Price	Sale Price	Profit

Total

Purchase & Sales Tracker

DATES FROM ________________

Item	Purchase Date	Sale Date	Sale Website	Purchase Price	Sale Price	Profit

Total

Purchase & Sales Tracker

Item	Purchase Date	Sale Date	Sale Website	Purchase Price	Sale Price	Profit

Total

Purchase & Sales Tracker

DATES FROM _______________

Item	Purchase Date	Sale Date	Sale Website	Purchase Price	Sale Price	Profit

Total

Purchase & Sales Tracker

Item	Purchase Date	Sale Date	Sale Website	Purchase Price	Sale Price	Profit

Total

Purchase & Sales Tracker

DATES FROM _______________

Item	Purchase Date	Sale Date	Sale Website	Purchase Price	Sale Price	Profit

Total

Purchase & Sales Tracker

DATES FROM ______________

Item	Purchase Date	Sale Date	Sale Website	Purchase Price	Sale Price	Profit

Total

Purchase & Sales Tracker

DATES FROM ___________________

Item	Purchase Date	Sale Date	Sale Website	Purchase Price	Sale Price	Profit

Total

Purchase & Sales Tracker

Item	Purchase Date	Sale Date	Sale Website	Purchase Price	Sale Price	Profit

	Total			

Purchase & Sales Tracker

DATES FROM _______________

Item	Purchase Date	Sale Date	Sale Website	Purchase Price	Sale Price	Profit

Total ____________

Purchase & Sales Tracker

DATES FROM ___________________

Item	Purchase Date	Sale Date	Sale Website	Purchase Price	Sale Price	Profit

Total

Purchase & Sales Tracker

Item	Purchase Date	Sale Date	Sale Website	Purchase Price	Sale Price	Profit

Total

Purchase & Sales Tracker

DATES FROM ______________________

Item	Purchase Date	Sale Date	Sale Website	Purchase Price	Sale Price	Profit

Total

Purchase & Sales Tracker

Item	Purchase Date	Sale Date	Sale Website	Purchase Price	Sale Price	Profit

Total

Purchase & Sales Tracker

Item	Purchase Date	Sale Date	Sale Website	Purchase Price	Sale Price	Profit

Total

Purchase & Sales Tracker

DATES FROM _______________

Item	Purchase Date	Sale Date	Sale Website	Purchase Price	Sale Price	Profit

Total

Purchase & Sales Tracker

DATES FROM ______________________

Item	Purchase Date	Sale Date	Sale Website	Purchase Price	Sale Price	Profit

Total

Purchase & Sales Tracker

DATES FROM ______________________

Item	Purchase Date	Sale Date	Sale Website	Purchase Price	Sale Price	Profit

Total

Purchase & Sales Tracker

DATES FROM ______________

Item	Purchase Date	Sale Date	Sale Website	Purchase Price	Sale Price	Profit

Total ______________

Purchase & Sales Tracker

DATES FROM ________________________

Item	Purchase Date	Sale Date	Sale Website	Purchase Price	Sale Price	Profit

Total | | | |